SUSHI AT

Essential Recipes, Pro Tips, and Mistakes to Avoid for Perfect Homemade Sushi

Copyright © 2024 O.Naumchyk
All rights reserved. No part of this book may be reproduced, distributed, or transmitted in any form or by any means, including photocopying, recording, or other electronic or mechanical methods, without the prior written permission of the author, except as allowed by copyright law.
Every image, design, and piece of content within this book is safeguarded by copyright and is the sole property of the author.

Contents of the book:

Introduction: Welcome to the Art of Sushi at Home
1-4

Chapter 1: The World of Sushi and Rolls
5-12

Chapter 2: Classic sushi and roll recipes
13-28

Chapter 3: Recipes for making baked sushi and rolls at home
29-40

Chapter 4: Recipes for vegetarian sushi rolls and nigiri
41-50

Chapter 5: Practical tips and life hacks to improve your sushi-making skills
51-56

Chapter 6: Common mistakes people make when making sushi and rolls at home
57-62

Chapter 7: Fusion Roll Recipes
63-70

Final Thoughts: Becoming a Sushi Artisan at Home
71-72

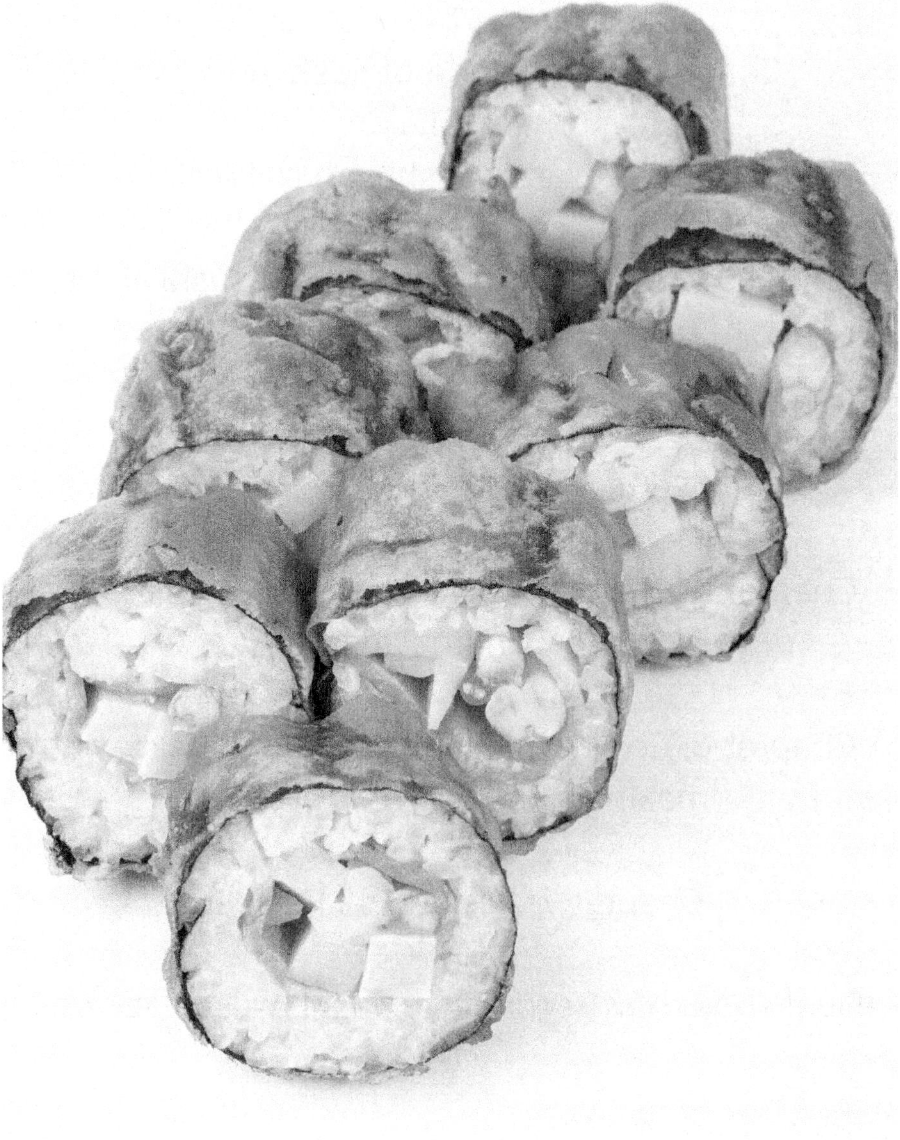

Introduction: Welcome to the Art of Sushi at Home

There's something truly magical about sushi. From its origins in Japanese tradition to its modern-day popularity worldwide, sushi has become an art form that combines fresh, high-quality ingredients with skill, precision, and creativity. Whether it's the elegant simplicity of a slice of fish atop seasoned rice, the vibrant colors of a rainbow roll, or the savory warmth of a baked sushi casserole, sushi invites us to savor each bite with intention and appreciation.

But sushi isn't just for restaurant tables and skilled chefs—this book is here to show you that with a few essential techniques, the right ingredients, and a touch of practice, you can bring the beauty and flavor of sushi into your own kitchen. Imagine the satisfaction of crafting your first nigiri, rolling your first maki, or creating your own signature roll, all from the comfort of home. This book is designed to guide you through that journey, from the basics to more advanced styles and techniques.

What You'll Discover in This Book
In Sushi at Home: Master the Art of Sushi and Rolls, you'll find everything you need to get started with homemade sushi:

Essential Ingredients and Tools: Learn about the key ingredients and tools that make sushi possible—from sushi-grade fish and nori to bamboo mats and rice cookers. Each item has a role in creating authentic, delicious sushi.

Sushi Rice Preparation: Perfecting sushi rice is at the heart of great sushi. This book will guide you through the steps to achieve that slightly sticky, perfectly seasoned rice that holds everything together.

Detailed Recipes: With recipes, you'll explore classic nigiri and maki rolls, innovative vegetarian options, warm baked sushi, and creative fusion rolls. Each recipe includes step-by-step instructions, helpful tips, and variations to inspire your creativity.

Common Mistakes and How to Avoid Them: Even seasoned sushi makers encounter challenges. We'll walk you through common mistakes and simple fixes to help you succeed every step of the way.

Who This Book is For

Whether you're a complete beginner looking to explore Japanese cuisine or a sushi lover aiming to recreate your favorite rolls at home, this book is for you. Each chapter builds on the last, taking you from the foundational skills of choosing ingredients and preparing rice to crafting beautiful, delicious rolls that will impress family and friends.

A Delicious Journey Awaits

Making sushi at home is a blend of skill and

creativity, tradition and experimentation. It's a process that rewards patience and practice but allows you to play with flavors, textures, and presentation. You're about to embark on a culinary adventure that will bring you joy, satisfaction, and the pleasure of sharing your creations with others. So, sharpen your knives, gather your ingredients, and let's roll into the art of sushi!

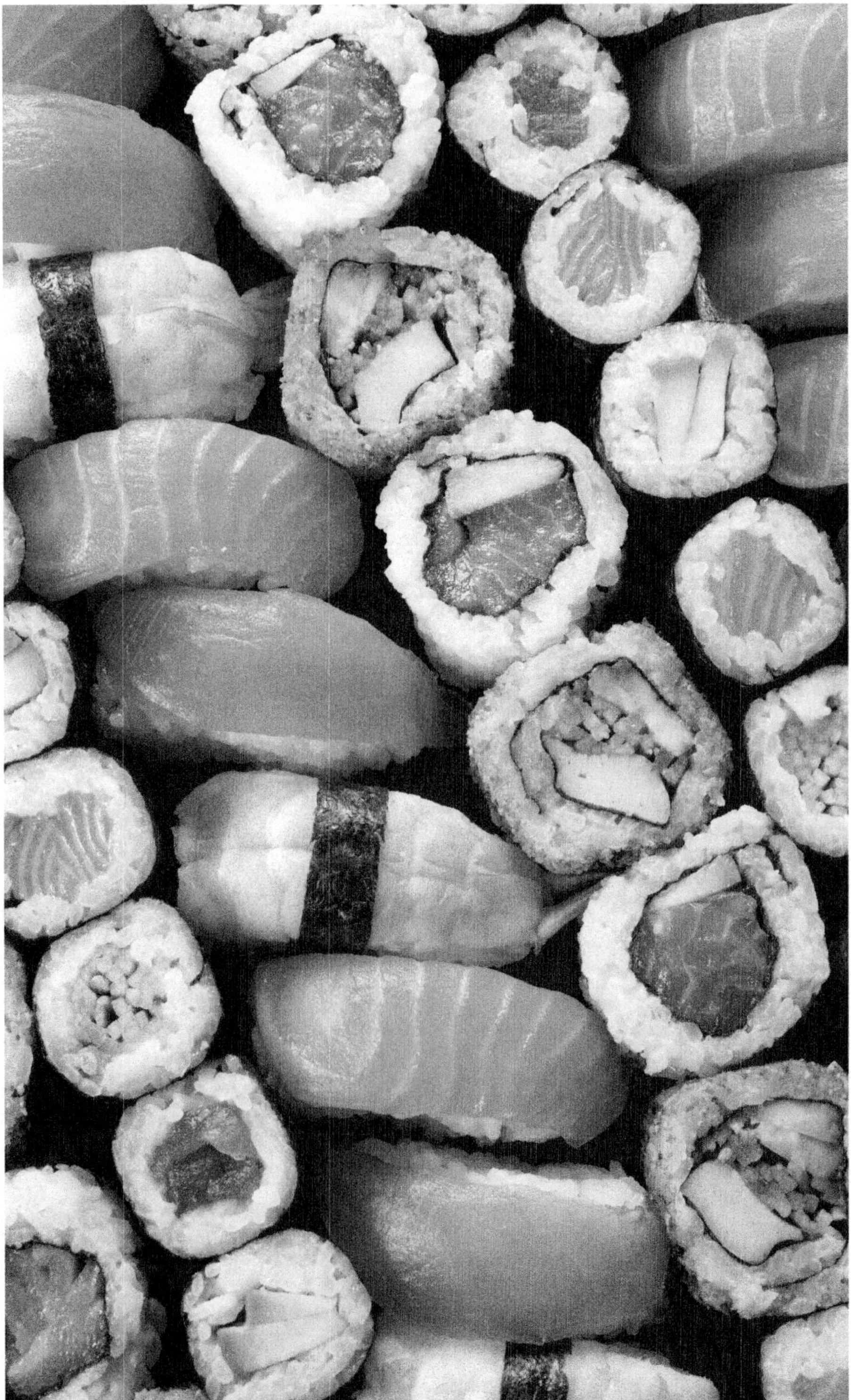

Chapter 1: The World of Sushi and Rolls

Sushi and rolls have captured the culinary hearts of people around the world. They are celebrated not just for their taste and unique textures but also for the skill and precision involved in their creation. This chapter takes you on a journey through the origins of sushi and rolls, introduces you to the essential ingredients and tools, and guides you through the foundational techniques needed to make sushi at home.

1.1 The Origins and History of Sushi

Sushi has a rich history that dates back centuries. Originally, sushi did not resemble the sushi we know today; it began as a method of preserving fish in fermented rice. This technique, called narezushi, originated in Southeast Asia and made its way to Japan around the 8th century. In Japan, the fish was cleaned, salted, and then pressed in rice to ferment, allowing it to last for several months. The rice was discarded, and only the fish was consumed.

By the Edo period (1603-1868), sushi had evolved into hayazushi (meaning "fast sushi"), where both fish and rice were consumed. With the growth of Tokyo (formerly Edo) as a bustling city, fast food became popular. It was during this period that nigiri sushi emerged, made with fresh fish and vinegared rice, rather than fermented fish and rice. This style was convenient, delicious, and could be eaten on the go, much like today's sushi.

Over time, various styles of sushi developed, such as maki (rolled sushi) and temaki (hand rolls), and sushi continued to evolve as it spread globally.

1.2 Types of Sushi and Rolls

There are several popular types of sushi and rolls, each with unique characteristics. Here's a breakdown:

Nigiri: A small, oblong mound of vinegared rice with a slice of fish or seafood placed on top. It's often garnished with a dab of wasabi or a thin band of nori (seaweed).

Sashimi: Technically not a type of sushi, sashimi refers to thinly sliced raw fish or seafood, served without rice.

Maki (Rolls): These are rolls made with rice and various fillings, wrapped in a sheet of nori and sliced into bite-sized pieces. Common types of maki include:

Hosomaki: Thin rolls with a single filling, such as cucumber or tuna.

Futomaki: Thicker rolls with multiple fillings, often colorful and complex.

Uramaki: Inside-out rolls with rice on the outside, such as the popular California roll.

Temaki (Hand Rolls): Cone-shaped rolls filled with rice, fish, and vegetables. These are eaten by hand and are typically larger than maki.

Chirashi (Scattered Sushi): A bowl of sushi rice topped with various sashimi and garnishes. This style of sushi is less structured and allows for a mix of textures and flavors.

Oshizushi (Pressed Sushi): Made by layering rice and fish in a box mold and pressing it into a rectangular shape before slicing. It's a specialty of the Kansai region.

Each type offers a different experience in terms of texture, presentation, and flavor.

1.3 Choosing the Right Rice for Sushi

The foundation of any good sushi is the rice. Japanese short-grain rice is traditionally used for sushi because of its sticky, slightly chewy texture, which holds well when shaped. Here are a few important points about sushi rice:

Type: Look for Japanese short-grain or medium-grain rice, often labeled as "sushi rice" in stores.

Texture: Sushi rice should have a sticky, glossy finish once cooked, which helps it bind together.

Flavoring: Rice vinegar, sugar, and salt are mixed into the cooked rice to give it the signature sushi flavor. This mixture is known as "sushi-zu."

1.4 Essential Ingredients for Sushi

To make sushi, you'll need a few basic ingredients:

Sushi Rice: As discussed, this is the base of all sushi types.

Nori (Seaweed Sheets): Thin, dried sheets of seaweed are used for wrapping maki rolls and some nigiri.

Fish and Seafood: Freshness is key. Common choices include tuna, salmon, yellowtail, shrimp, and eel. Some of the fish used should be sushi-grade to ensure safety when eaten raw.

Vegetables: Cucumbers, avocados, carrots, and radishes are popular for adding crunch and color.

Condiments and Sauces:

Soy Sauce: Often used for dipping.

Wasabi: A green paste with a strong, spicy flavor that complements raw fish.

Pickled Ginger (Gari): Served as a palate cleanser between different types of sushi.

1.5 Cooking Rice for Sushi

Making perfect sushi rice takes some attention to detail. Here's a step-by-step guide:

Rinse the Rice: Place the rice in a bowl and rinse it under cold water until the water runs clear. This removes excess starch, which can make the rice too sticky.

Soak: After rinsing, soak the rice in water for about 30 minutes. This allows the grains to absorb water evenly.

Cook: Use a rice cooker for consistent results, or cook on the stovetop. For stovetop cooking, bring the rice and water to a boil, then reduce heat to low, cover, and simmer for about 15 minutes. Let it sit, covered, for an additional 10 minutes after cooking.

Season: Gently fold a mixture of rice vinegar, sugar,

and salt (sushi-zu) into the warm rice. Use a wooden spoon to mix carefully to avoid breaking the grains.
Cool: Spread the rice in a thin layer to cool it. Traditionally, a fan is used to cool the rice quickly, giving it a glossy finish.

1.6 Other Essential Ingredients

In addition to the basic ingredients, certain items are frequently used for making rolls and enhancing flavors:

Sesame Seeds: Often sprinkled on the outside of uramaki (inside-out rolls) for added texture.
Tempura Batter: Adds a crispy texture when used with vegetables or shrimp.
Spicy Mayo: A mixture of mayonnaise and Sriracha, used as a topping for some rolls.
Eel Sauce (Unagi Sauce): A sweet soy-based sauce often drizzled on rolls with eel.

1.7 Essential Tools for Sushi Making

To make sushi at home, a few specialized tools can make the process easier:

Bamboo Mat (Makisu): Used for rolling maki. Wrap it in plastic wrap to prevent sticking.
Sharp Knife: A sharp knife is essential for cutting clean slices of fish and neatly slicing rolls.
Rice Paddle (Shamoji): Used for mixing and spreading the sushi rice.
Rice Cooker: Optional, but very useful for consistent rice preparation.

1.8 Making Sushi at Home: A Step-by-Step Guide

Making sushi at home can be a fun and rewarding experience.

Here's a basic outline to get started with a simple maki roll:

Prepare the Ingredients: Slice your fish and vegetables into thin, even pieces.

Prepare the Rice: Follow the instructions in section 1.5 to make your sushi rice.

Place the Nori on the Mat: Lay a sheet of nori on your bamboo mat with the shiny side down.

Spread the Rice: Wet your hands to prevent sticking and spread a thin layer of rice over the nori, leaving a small border at the top.

Add Fillings: Place your fillings (e.g., fish, cucumber, avocado) in a line across the center of the rice.
Roll: Lift the edge of the mat closest to you, and start rolling tightly, keeping the fillings centered. Apply gentle pressure to shape the roll as you go.

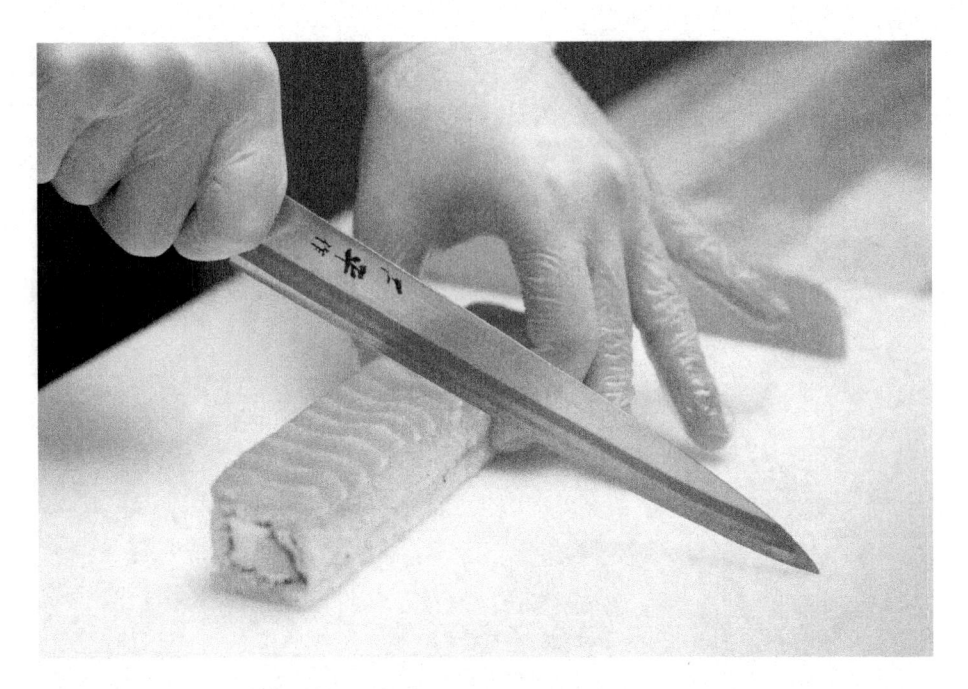

Slice: Use a sharp, wet knife to cut the roll into bite-sized pieces.
Serve and Enjoy: Arrange your sushi on a plate and serve with soy sauce, wasabi, and pickled ginger.

Summary
In this chapter, we explored the origins of sushi, the various types, and the importance of choosing the right ingredients, especially sushi rice. We also covered essential tools and techniques for making sushi at home. Sushi-making is both an art and a skill, so practice and patience are key.

Chapter 2: Classic sushi and roll recipes

Recipe 1: Classic Nigiri Sushi
Description: Nigiri sushi is a simple and elegant type of sushi made with hand-pressed vinegared rice topped with a thin slice of fish or seafood.

Ingredients:
1 cup sushi rice (short-grain Japanese rice)
1 cup water
2 tbsp rice vinegar
1 tbsp sugar
1/2 tsp salt
200g sushi-grade fish (salmon, tuna, or yellowtail)
Wasabi paste
Soy sauce, for serving
Pickled ginger, for serving

Method:
Prepare the Rice:
Rinse the rice thoroughly until water runs clear. Soak for 30 minutes, then cook in a rice cooker with water.
Once cooked, mix rice vinegar, sugar, and salt in a small saucepan over low heat until dissolved, then fold it into the rice.
Prepare the Fish:
Using a very sharp knife, slice the fish into thin, even pieces about 2 inches long and 1/2 inch thick.

Form the Nigiri:
Wet your hands with water to prevent rice from sticking. Take a small portion of rice and shape it into an oblong ball.
Place a small dab of wasabi on the rice and gently press a slice of fish on top.
Serve:
Arrange nigiri on a platter, serving with soy sauce, pickled ginger, and wasabi.

Recipe 2: California Roll (Inside-Out Roll)
Description: A popular roll with crab, avocado, and cucumber, rolled with rice on the outside.

Ingredients:
1 cup sushi rice, prepared as above
3 sheets of nori
100g imitation crab or real crab meat

1 avocado, sliced
1 cucumber, julienned
2 tbsp mayonnaise
1 tbsp sesame seeds

Method:
Prepare the Crab Filling:
Mix crab with mayonnaise for a creamy filling.
Roll the Sushi:
Place a bamboo mat covered in plastic wrap on a flat surface. Lay a nori sheet on the mat, shiny side down.
Spread a thin layer of rice over the nori, then sprinkle with sesame seeds. Flip the sheet so the rice side is down.
Arrange crab mixture, avocado slices, and cucumber sticks along the bottom edge of the nori.
Roll tightly using the mat, then slice into bite-sized pieces.
Serve:
Serve California rolls with soy sauce and wasabi.

Recipe 3: Spicy Tuna Roll

Description: This roll combines tuna with a spicy, creamy sauce and is wrapped in rice and nori.

Ingredients:
1 cup sushi rice, prepared
3 sheets of nori
200g sushi-grade tuna, diced
2 tbsp mayonnaise
1 tbsp Sriracha or hot sauce
1 cucumber, julienned

Method:
Make the Spicy Tuna Mixture:
In a bowl, mix diced tuna with mayonnaise and Sriracha to taste.
Roll the Sushi:
Place a nori sheet on a bamboo mat, spread rice evenly, and flip it over.
Add a line of spicy tuna and cucumber along one edge of the nori.
Roll tightly and slice.
Serve:
Serve with soy sauce, wasabi, and pickled ginger.

Recipe 4: Vegetable Tempura Roll
Description: A crunchy vegetarian roll with tempura-battered vegetables.

Ingredients:
1 cup sushi rice, prepared
3 sheets of nori
Tempura batter mix
1/2 sweet potato, julienned
1/2 bell pepper, julienned
1/2 zucchini, julienned

Method:
Prepare Tempura Vegetables:
Coat vegetables in tempura batter and fry until golden and crisp. Drain on paper towels.
Assemble the Roll:
Place rice on nori, flip, and arrange tempura

vegetables in a line.
Roll tightly, slice, and serve.
Serve:
Serve with a drizzle of eel sauce or soy sauce.

Recipe 5: Rainbow Roll
Description: A colorful roll topped with various types of fish, representing a rainbow.
Ingredients:
1 cup sushi rice, prepared
3 sheets of nori
100g imitation crab or real crab meat, mixed with mayo
1 avocado, sliced
Assorted sushi-grade fish (salmon, tuna, yellowtail, shrimp)
Cucumber, julienned

Method:
Prepare the Base Roll:
Place rice on nori, flip, and add crab mixture, cucumber, and avocado.
Roll tightly.
Top with Fish:
Layer thin slices of various fish on top of the roll, then gently press to secure.
Slice carefully, keeping toppings intact.
Serve:
Serve with soy sauce, wasabi, and pickled ginger.

Recipe 6: Tekka Maki (Tuna Roll)
Description: Tekka Maki is a simple, classic roll made with sushi-grade tuna. The flavor of fresh tuna shines through with minimal ingredients.
Ingredients:
1 cup sushi rice, prepared as above
1 sheet nori
100g sushi-grade tuna, sliced into thin strips
Wasabi (optional)

Method:
Lay a sheet of nori on the bamboo mat, spread a thin layer of rice, and leave a 1-inch gap at the top. Place a strip of tuna and a dab of wasabi along the rice.
Roll tightly and slice.

Tips:
Ensure the tuna is fresh and sushi-grade.
Wet knife for clean slices.
Serving Suggestions: Serve with soy sauce and wasabi.

Recipe 7: Philadelphia Roll
Description: Known for its creamy flavor, the Philadelphia Roll combines smoked salmon, cream cheese, and cucumber.

Ingredients:
1 cup sushi rice, prepared
1 sheet nori
80g smoked salmon
2 tbsp cream cheese
1 cucumber, julienned

Method:
Lay nori on a bamboo mat, spread rice, flip over. Arrange salmon, cream cheese, and cucumber along the edge.
Roll tightly and slice.

Tips:
Use softened cream cheese for easy spreading.
Serve chilled for the best texture.
Serving Suggestions: Serve with soy sauce and pickled ginger.

Recipe 8: Shrimp Tempura Roll

Description: This roll features crunchy shrimp tempura with creamy avocado and cucumber.

Ingredients:
1 cup sushi rice, prepared
1 sheet nori
2 shrimp tempura (pre-made or homemade)
1/2 avocado, sliced
1 cucumber, julienned

Method:
Place nori on mat, spread rice, flip over.
Add shrimp, avocado, and cucumber, roll tightly, and slice.
Tips:
Keep tempura crispy by serving immediately.
Use fresh oil for frying shrimp tempura.
Serving Suggestions: Serve with eel sauce for a sweet flavor.

Recipe 9: Spicy Salmon Roll
Description: This roll combines fresh salmon with a spicy kick from Sriracha.
Ingredients:
1 cup sushi rice, prepared
1 sheet nori
150g sushi-grade salmon, diced

1 tbsp mayonnaise
1 tsp Sriracha
1 cucumber, julienned

Method:
Mix diced salmon, mayonnaise, and Sriracha.
Lay nori on mat, spread rice, flip, add filling, and roll.
Tips:
Adjust Sriracha to taste.
Fresh cucumber adds crunch.
Serving Suggestions: Serve with soy sauce and wasabi.

Recipe 10: Yellowtail Scallion Roll
Description: A delicate roll with yellowtail and fresh scallions.

Ingredients:
1 cup sushi rice, prepared
1 sheet nori
100g yellowtail (hamachi), thinly sliced
2 scallions, chopped

Method:
Lay nori on mat, spread rice, flip over.
Place yellowtail and scallions, roll, and slice.
Tips:
Use fresh, high-quality yellowtail.
Chop scallions finely for a subtle flavor.
Serving Suggestions: Serve with soy sauce and lemon zest.

Recipe 11: Spicy Scallop Roll

Description: Creamy scallops mixed with spicy mayo for a luxurious flavor.

Ingredients:
1 cup sushi rice, prepared
1 sheet nori
150g scallops, chopped
1 tbsp mayonnaise
1/2 tsp Sriracha

Method:
Mix scallops with mayo and Sriracha.
Lay nori, spread rice, add filling, and roll.

Tips:
Use fresh scallops.
Adjust Sriracha for desired heat.
Serving Suggestions: Serve with lemon wedges and soy sauce.

Recipe 12: Dragon Roll

Description: This roll combines grilled eel with cucumber and is topped with avocado.

Ingredients:
1 cup sushi rice, prepared
1 sheet nori
100g grilled eel (unagi)
1/2 avocado, thinly sliced
1 cucumber, julienned
Eel sauce for drizzling

Method:
Lay nori on mat, spread rice, add eel and cucumber, and roll.
Top with avocado slices, press gently, and slice.
Tips:
Drizzle eel sauce generously for flavor.
Arrange avocado for a "dragon" appearance.
Serving Suggestions: Serve with extra eel sauce and sesame seeds.

Recipe 13: Spider Roll

Description: Features crispy soft-shell crab with cucumber and avocado.

Ingredients:
1 cup sushi rice, prepared
1 sheet nori
1 soft-shell crab, fried
1 cucumber, julienned
1/2 avocado, sliced

Method:
Place nori on mat, spread rice, add crab and vegetables, and roll.

Tips:
Fry crab until crispy.
Serve immediately for texture.
Serving Suggestions: Serve with soy sauce and spicy mayo.

Recipe 14: Boston Roll

Description: An American-inspired roll with poached shrimp, lettuce, and cucumber.

Ingredients:
1 cup sushi rice, prepared
1 sheet nori
100g poached shrimp
1 lettuce leaf
1 cucumber, julienned

Method:
Place nori on mat, spread rice, add shrimp, lettuce, and cucumber, and roll.

Tips:
Use fresh, high-quality shrimp.
Serve chilled.
Serving Suggestions: Serve with soy sauce and pickled ginger.

Chapter 3: Recipes for making baked sushi and rolls at home

Recipe 1: Baked California Roll Casserole
Description: A deconstructed California roll in a creamy, baked form.
Ingredients:
2 cups sushi rice, cooked and seasoned
1 cup imitation crab, shredded
1 avocado, diced
1/2 cup mayonnaise
1 tbsp Sriracha (optional)
1 tbsp soy sauce
2 tbsp furikake (Japanese seasoning)
1 sheet nori, shredded for garnish

Method:
Preheat oven to 375°F (190°C).
In a mixing bowl, combine shredded crab, mayonnaise, Sriracha, and soy sauce.
Spread seasoned sushi rice evenly in a baking dish, then sprinkle with furikake.
Layer the crab mixture and diced avocado over the rice.
Bake for 15 minutes or until the top is slightly golden.
Garnish with shredded nori and serve with soy sauce.
Tips:
Adjust Sriracha for spiciness.
Add more furikake for extra flavor.
Serving Suggestion: Serve with a spoon to scoop onto seaweed or enjoy as a casserole.

Recipe 2: Baked Spicy Salmon Roll
Description: Spicy salmon and creamy sauce baked into a roll for a warm, hearty experience.

Ingredients:
2 cups sushi rice, prepared
200g salmon, diced
1/2 cup mayonnaise
1 tbsp Sriracha
1 tbsp green onions, chopped
2 tbsp sesame seeds
3 sheets of nori

Method:
Preheat oven to 400°F (200°C).
Mix salmon, mayo, Sriracha, and green onions.
Spread rice on nori, add salmon mix, roll, and cut into pieces.
Arrange rolls in a baking dish, sprinkle with sesame seeds, and bake for 10-15 minutes.
Tips:
For crispier edges, broil for 2 minutes.
Adjust Sriracha for spice level.
Serving Suggestion: Serve warm with soy sauce or eel sauce.

Recipe 3: Baked Eel Avocado Roll
Description: A savory baked roll featuring eel and creamy avocado.
Ingredients:
2 cups sushi rice, prepared

100g grilled eel (unagi), sliced
1 avocado, diced
3 sheets of nori
2 tbsp eel sauce

Method:
Preheat oven to 375°F (190°C).
Spread rice on nori, place eel and avocado, roll, and cut into pieces.
Arrange rolls in a baking dish and drizzle with eel sauce.
Bake for 10-12 minutes or until lightly crispy.
Tips:
Brush more eel sauce on top before serving.
Keep avocado slices small for even baking.
Serving Suggestion: Serve with extra eel sauce.

Recipe 4: Baked Volcano Roll

Description: A spicy roll topped with baked scallops, shrimp, and creamy sauce for a volcanic burst of flavor.

Ingredients:

2 cups sushi rice, prepared
3 sheets of nori
1/2 cup imitation crab, shredded
1/2 cup scallops, chopped
1/2 cup shrimp, chopped
1/2 cup mayonnaise
1 tbsp Sriracha
1 tbsp green onions, chopped

Method:

Preheat oven to 400°F (200°C).
In a bowl, mix crab, scallops, shrimp, mayo, and Sriracha.
Spread rice on nori, roll, slice, and arrange in a baking dish.
Spoon seafood mixture over each roll and bake for 10-15 minutes.

Tips:
Broil for extra browning.
Adjust Sriracha for spiciness.
Serving Suggestion: Garnish with green onions.

Recipe 5: Baked Spicy Tuna Casserole

Description: Deconstructed spicy tuna in casserole form with creamy, baked topping.

Ingredients:
2 cups sushi rice, prepared
200g sushi-grade tuna, diced
1/2 cup mayonnaise
1 tbsp Sriracha
1 tbsp soy sauce
1 tbsp sesame seeds
2 sheets nori, shredded for garnish

Method:
Preheat oven to 375°F (190°C).
Mix tuna, mayo, Sriracha, and soy sauce.
Spread rice in a baking dish, add tuna mixture on top, and sprinkle with sesame seeds.
Bake for 15-20 minutes or until golden.

Tips:
Broil for a crispy top.
Add extra sesame seeds for flavor.
Serving Suggestion: Serve with seaweed on the side.

Recipe 6: Baked Crab Roll

Description: A baked roll with creamy crab filling.

Ingredients:
2 cups sushi rice, prepared
1 cup imitation crab, shredded
1/2 cup mayonnaise

1 tbsp furikake
3 sheets nori

Method:
Preheat oven to 375°F (190°C).
Spread rice on nori, add crab mix, roll, slice, and arrange in a baking dish.
Sprinkle with furikake and bake for 10-15 minutes.
Tips:
Serve with extra furikake.
Avoid over-baking for tender crab.
Serving Suggestion: Serve with soy sauce.

Recipe 7: Baked Dynamite Roll
Description: A baked roll with spicy tuna and creamy sauce for an explosion of flavor.
Ingredients:
2 cups sushi rice, prepared

1/2 cup tuna, diced
1/2 cup mayonnaise
1 tbsp Sriracha
2 tbsp green onions, chopped
3 sheets of nori

Method:
Preheat oven to 400°F (200°C).
Spread rice on nori, add tuna mix, roll, slice, and place in a baking dish.
Bake for 10-15 minutes until golden.
Tips:
Serve with extra Sriracha.
Adjust green onions to taste.
Serving Suggestion: Garnish with green onions.

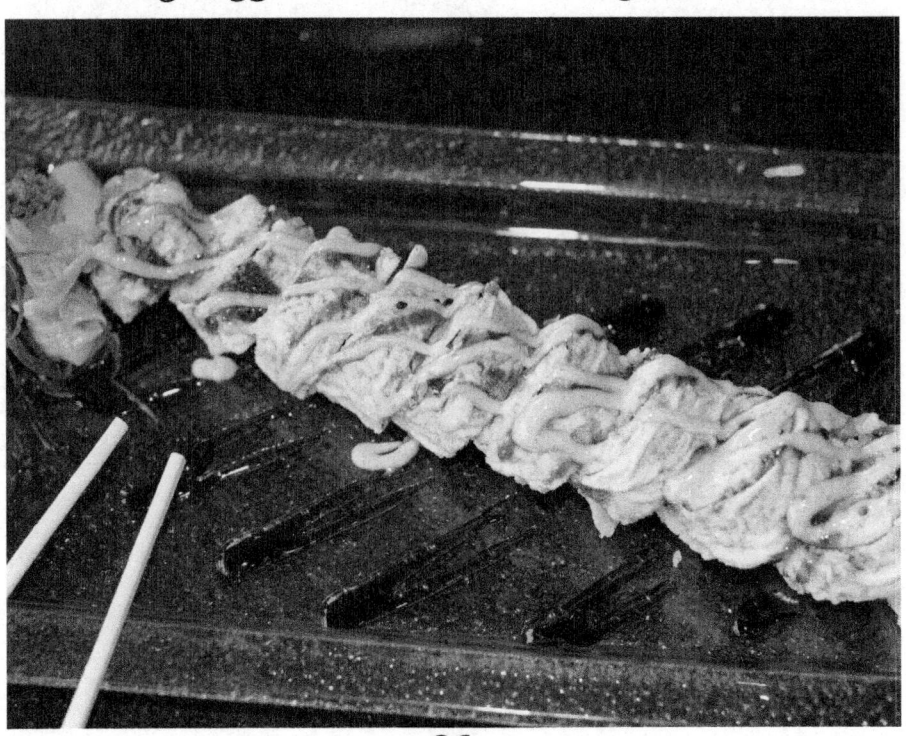

Recipe 8: Baked Salmon Teriyaki Roll

Description: A savory roll featuring salmon glazed with teriyaki sauce.

Ingredients:
2 cups sushi rice, prepared
200g salmon, sliced
2 tbsp teriyaki sauce
1/2 avocado, sliced
3 sheets nori

Method:
Preheat oven to 375°F (190°C).
Spread rice on nori, add salmon and avocado, roll, slice, and place in a baking dish.
Drizzle with teriyaki sauce and bake for 10-12 minutes.

Tips:
Add extra teriyaki for flavor.
Avoid over-baking to keep avocado tender.
Serving Suggestion: Serve with soy sauce.

Recipe 9: Baked Shrimp Tempura Roll

Description: A warm twist on shrimp tempura roll.

Ingredients:
2 cups sushi rice, prepared
4 shrimp tempura, pre-cooked
1/2 avocado, sliced
3 sheets nori
2 tbsp eel sauce

Method:
Preheat oven to 375°F (190°C).
Spread rice on nori, place shrimp and avocado, roll, slice, and arrange in a baking dish.
Drizzle with eel sauce and bake for 10 minutes.
Tips:
Broil for a crispier texture.
Add extra eel sauce for flavor.
Serving Suggestion: Serve warm with soy sauce.

Recipe 10: Baked Creamy Crab and Cheese Roll
Description: A rich, creamy roll with crab and cheese.
Ingredients:
2 cups sushi rice, prepared
1 cup imitation crab, shredded
1/2 cup cream cheese
1/4 cup mayonnaise
3 sheets nori

Method:

Preheat oven to 375°F (190°C).

Spread rice on nori, add crab and cream cheese, roll, slice, and place in a baking dish.

Bake for 10-12 minutes until warm and creamy.

Tips:

Avoid over-baking the cream cheese.

Use cold cream cheese for easier slicing.

Serving Suggestion: Serve with soy sauce.

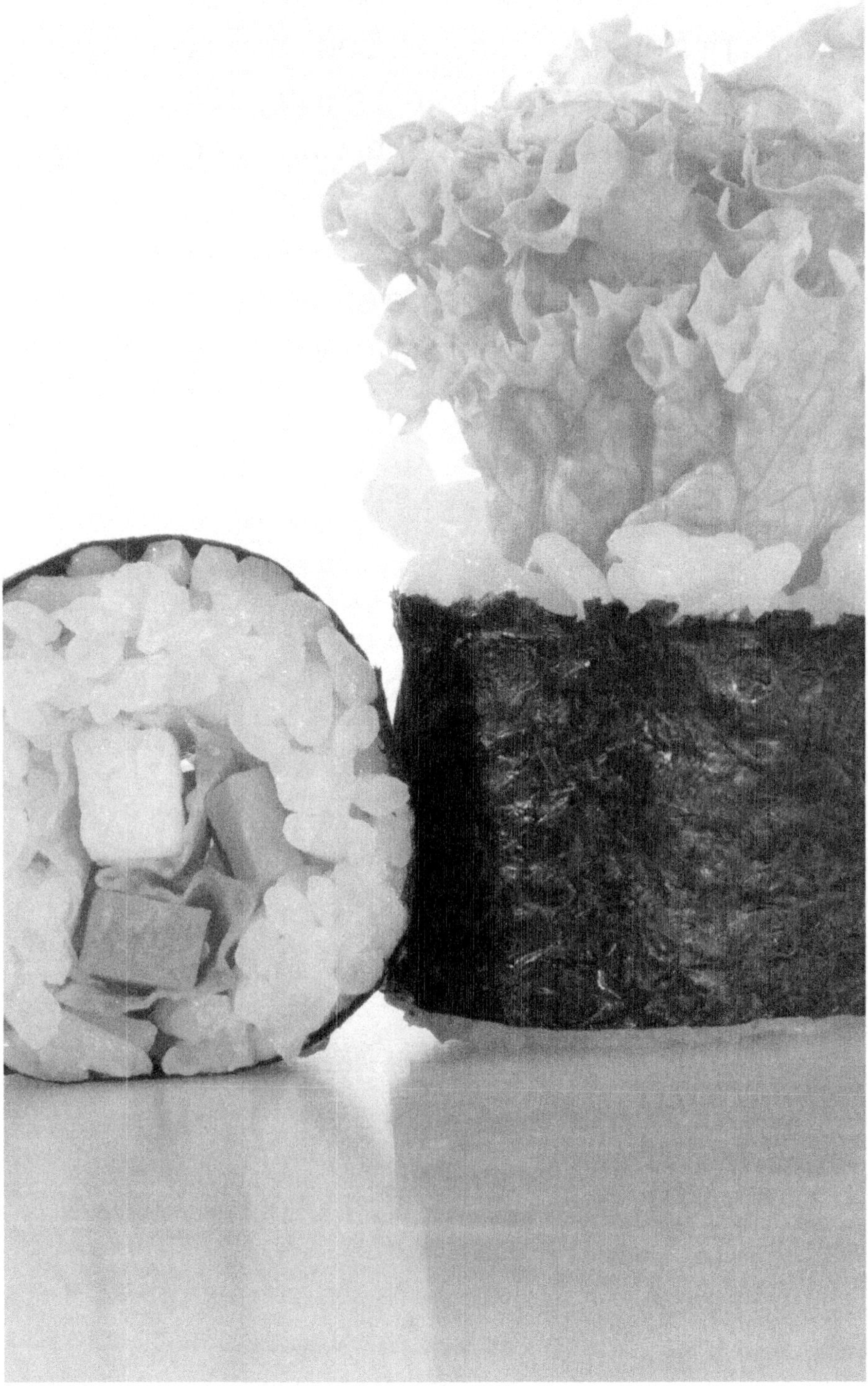

Chapter 4: Recipes for vegetarian sushi rolls and nigiri

These recipes are entirely plant-based, showcasing fresh vegetables, fruits, and creative ingredients to replace traditional fish.

Recipe 1: Avocado Cucumber Roll
Description: A refreshing and creamy roll featuring avocado and cucumber, perfect for a light bite.
Ingredients:
1 cup sushi rice, prepared and seasoned
1 sheet nori
1/2 avocado, sliced
1/2 cucumber, julienned
Sesame seeds, for garnish

Method:
Place the nori sheet on a bamboo mat with the shiny side down. Spread a thin layer of rice evenly over the nori, leaving a 1-inch gap at the top.

Place avocado slices and cucumber in a line across the rice.

Roll tightly, applying gentle pressure with the bamboo mat.

Slice into bite-sized pieces and sprinkle with sesame seeds.

Tips:

Keep avocado slices thin for easier rolling.

Wet the knife between cuts for clean slices.

Serving Suggestion: Serve with soy sauce and wasabi.

Recipe 2: Sweet Potato Tempura Roll
Description: A crunchy roll with tempura-battered sweet potato for a mix of sweetness and crispiness.

Ingredents:
1 cup sushi rice, prepared
1 sheet nori
1 small sweet potato, cut into thin strips
Tempura batter mix
Oil for frying
Sesame seeds for garnish

Method:
Prepare tempura batter according to package instructions and dip sweet potato strips in the batter.
Fry sweet potato until golden and crispy, then drain on paper towels.
Place nori on the bamboo mat, spread rice over it, flip, and place sweet potato strips.
Roll tightly, slice, and sprinkle with sesame seeds.
Tips:
Serve immediately for maximum crunch.
Adjust frying temperature to prevent sogginess.
Serving Suggestion: Serve with a drizzle of eel sauce for added sweetness.

Recipe 3: Shiitake Mushroom Nigiri
Description: A simple yet savory nigiri with marinated shiitake mushrooms for a rich, umami flavor.

Ingredients:
1 cup sushi rice, prepared

6 shiitake mushrooms, stems removed
1 tbsp soy sauce
1 tbsp mirin
1/2 tsp sugar

Method:
Marinate mushrooms in soy sauce, mirin, and sugar for 10 minutes.
Sauté mushrooms in a pan over medium heat until softened and glossy.
Form rice into small mounds and place a mushroom cap on each.
Tips:
Cool mushrooms slightly before placing them on rice.
Use damp hands to shape the rice.
Serving Suggestion: Serve with pickled ginger.

Recipe 4: Carrot and Avocado Roll
Description: A simple, colorful roll combining crunchy carrots and creamy avocado.

Ingredients:
1 cup sushi rice, prepared
1 sheet nori
1/2 avocado, sliced
1 small carrot, julienned

Method:
Place nori on the bamboo mat, spread rice, flip, and place avocado and carrot in a line.

Roll tightly, slice, and serve.

Tips:

Julienne carrots thinly for a better texture.

Use a damp knife for clean cuts.

Serving Suggestion: Serve with soy sauce and pickled ginger.

Recipe 5: Asparagus Tempura Roll

Description: A flavorful roll with crispy asparagus tempura for added crunch.

Ingredients:
1 cup sushi rice, prepared

1 sheet nori

4-5 asparagus spears

Tempura batter mix
Oil for frying

Method:
Prepare tempura batter and dip asparagus, then fry until crispy.
Spread rice over nori, flip, place asparagus tempura, and roll tightly.
Slice and serve immediately.
Tips:
Serve immediately to enjoy the crispy tempura.
Use thin asparagus for even cooking.
Serving Suggestion: Serve with spicy mayo.

Recipe 6: Avocado Mango Roll
Description: A refreshing, sweet-savory roll with creamy avocado and juicy mango.

Ingredients:
1 cup sushi rice, prepared
1 sheet nori
1/2 avocado, sliced
1/2 mango, sliced

Method:
Place nori on a bamboo mat, spread rice, flip, and add avocado and mango slices.
Roll tightly and slice.
Tips:
Use ripe mango for optimal sweetness.

Keep avocado and mango slices thin for easy rolling.
Serving Suggestion: Serve with a light drizzle of ponzu sauce.

Recipe 7: Cucumber Roll (Kappa Maki)

Description: A classic, refreshing roll with cucumber for a crisp and clean flavor.
Ingredients:
1 cup sushi rice, prepared
1 sheet nori
1 cucumber, julienned

Method:

Place nori on the bamboo mat, spread rice evenly, leaving a gap at the top.
Place cucumber in a line across the center, roll tightly, and slice.

Tips:
Use a seedless cucumber for a firmer texture.
Cut cucumber thinly for even distribution.
Serving Suggestion: Serve with soy sauce.

Recipe 8: Bell Pepper and Cream Cheese Roll
Description: A vibrant roll with colorful bell pepper and creamy cheese for a smooth contrast.
Ingredients:
1 cup sushi rice, prepared
1 sheet nori
1/2 bell pepper, thinly sliced (use different colors for variety)
2 tbsp cream cheese

Method:
Place nori on a bamboo mat, spread rice, flip, and add bell pepper and cream cheese.
Roll tightly and slice.
Tips:
Soften cream cheese for easier spreading.
Use a variety of bell pepper colors for a colorful roll.
Serving Suggestion: Serve with soy sauce.

Recipe 9: Spinach and Sesame Roll
Description: A nutty roll with blanched spinach and sesame seeds, inspired by Japanese "goma-ae" salad.
Ingredients:
1 cup sushi rice, prepared

1 sheet nori
1/2 cup fresh spinach, blanched and drained
1 tbsp sesame seeds
1 tsp soy sauce

Method:
Toss spinach with soy sauce and sesame seeds.
Spread rice on nori, flip, and place spinach.
Roll tightly, slice, and serve.
Tips:
Squeeze out excess water from spinach.
Toast sesame seeds for extra flavor.
Serving Suggestion: Serve with soy sauce.

Recipe 10: Pickled Radish (Oshinko) Roll
Description: A traditional vegetarian roll with pickled radish (oshinko), which adds a tangy and slightly sweet flavor.

Ingredients:
1 cup sushi rice, prepared
1 sheet nori
1/2 cup pickled daikon radish (oshinko), sliced into thin strips

Method:
Place nori on a bamboo mat, spread rice evenly.
Lay oshinko along the center, roll tightly, and slice.
Tips:
Use a very sharp knife for clean cuts.

Oshinko is often bright yellow, adding a beautiful color to the roll.
Serving Suggestion: Serve with soy sauce and wasabi.
These 10 vegetarian sushi rolls and nigiri recipes offer a variety of flavors, textures, and colors that showcase the versatility of plant-based sushi. Whether you're craving something creamy, crunchy, tangy, or refreshing, these rolls are perfect for a delicious vegetarian sushi spread. Enjoy!

Chapter 5: Practical tips and life hacks to improve your sushi-making skills

1. Choose the Right Rice
Use short-grain Japanese rice specifically labeled as "sushi rice" for the best texture. It's stickier and holds together well.

2. Rinse the Rice Thoroughly
Rinse sushi rice until the water runs clear to remove excess starch. This prevents the rice from becoming overly sticky or mushy.

3. Soak the Rice Before Cooking
After rinsing, soak the rice in water for 20-30 minutes. This ensures even cooking and gives it the perfect chewy texture.

4. Perfect Rice-to-Water Ratio
Use a 1:1 ratio of rice to water (or slightly more water) when cooking. For stovetop cooking, bring to a boil, reduce heat, cover, and simmer for 15 minutes.

5. Cool the Rice Properly
After cooking, transfer rice to a large bowl and spread it out to cool. Use a fan to cool it quickly, giving it a glossy finish.

6. Season the Rice Correctly
Mix rice vinegar, sugar, and salt to make "sushi-zu." Gently fold it into the rice to avoid breaking the grains.

7. Avoid Over-Seasoning
Use a light hand when seasoning the rice, as too much vinegar can overpower the flavor of the fillings.

8. Keep Your Hands Wet
Wet your hands with water or lightly dip them in vinegar water when handling rice. This prevents rice from sticking to your hands.

9. Use a Sharp Knife
A sharp knife ensures clean cuts, especially when slicing rolls. A dull knife will crush the roll and make the filling spill out.

10. Dampen the Knife for Cutting Rolls
Wet the blade of your knife with water between cuts. This reduces friction and prevents rice from sticking.

11. Wrap the Bamboo Mat in Plastic Wrap
Wrapping your bamboo mat in plastic wrap keeps rice from sticking and makes cleanup easier, especially for inside-out rolls.

12. Spread Rice Thinly and Evenly
Use just enough rice to cover the nori in a thin layer. Too much rice will make rolls too thick and hard to roll.

13. Leave an Inch of Nori Exposed
Leave about an inch of nori without rice at the top edge. This helps seal the roll when you finish rolling.

14. Keep Fillings Minimal
Overfilling makes rolls harder to close and can cause the nori to tear. Use small, even amounts of fillings.

15. Use Fresh, High-Quality Ingredients
Sushi tastes best with fresh ingredients. Use sushi-grade fish and crisp vegetables to ensure great flavor and safety.

16. Master the Rolling Technique
Start rolling tightly from the edge closest to you, using the bamboo mat to guide the roll. Apply gentle, even pressure to shape it.

17. Make Inside-Out Rolls Easier
Sprinkle sesame seeds on the rice before flipping the nori for an inside-out roll. This adds texture and prevents sticking.

18. Slice Fish Properly for Nigiri
Use a sharp knife and slice fish at an angle, around 1/4 inch thick. This helps it sit on the rice mound and maximizes flavor.

19. Add Wasabi Sparingly
When making nigiri, use a tiny dab of wasabi between the fish and rice. It enhances flavor without overpowering the fish.

20. Store Nori Properly
Nori can go stale quickly. Keep it in an airtight container to preserve its crisp texture.

21. Use a Rice Paddle for Mixing
Use a rice paddle (shamoji) to gently fold vinegar into the rice. Avoid mashing or stirring too vigorously.

22. Toast Nori for Extra Crispiness
Lightly toast nori over a low flame for a few seconds

on each side to enhance its flavor and crispness.

23. Try Soy Paper as an Alternative
For those who don't like nori, use soy paper (mamenori) for a milder, colorful alternative to wrap your rolls.

24. Practice Rice Mounding for Nigiri
Form small, oblong mounds of rice by lightly pressing it with your fingers. Don't squeeze; the rice should hold shape but remain airy.

25. Chill Fish Before Slicing
Briefly chill fish in the freezer for about 15 minutes before slicing to make it firmer and easier to cut evenly.

26. Experiment with Different Sauces
Try eel sauce, ponzu, or spicy mayo to add variety. Drizzle lightly or serve on the side for dipping.

27. Add Tempura for Texture
Use tempura flakes (tentsuyu) as a filling or topping for added crunch and flavor, especially in rolls like the "Crunchy Roll."

28. Use a Clean Towel for Shape Correction
Gently press a damp, clean kitchen towel over a sliced roll if it needs reshaping after cutting.

29. Make a Dipping Sauce with Restraint
Sushi flavors are delicate. Use a light dip of soy sauce or ponzu to enhance flavors without overwhelming them.

30. Serve Immediately for Freshness
Sushi is best when eaten fresh. Serve rolls and nigiri

right after making them to enjoy the perfect texture and taste.

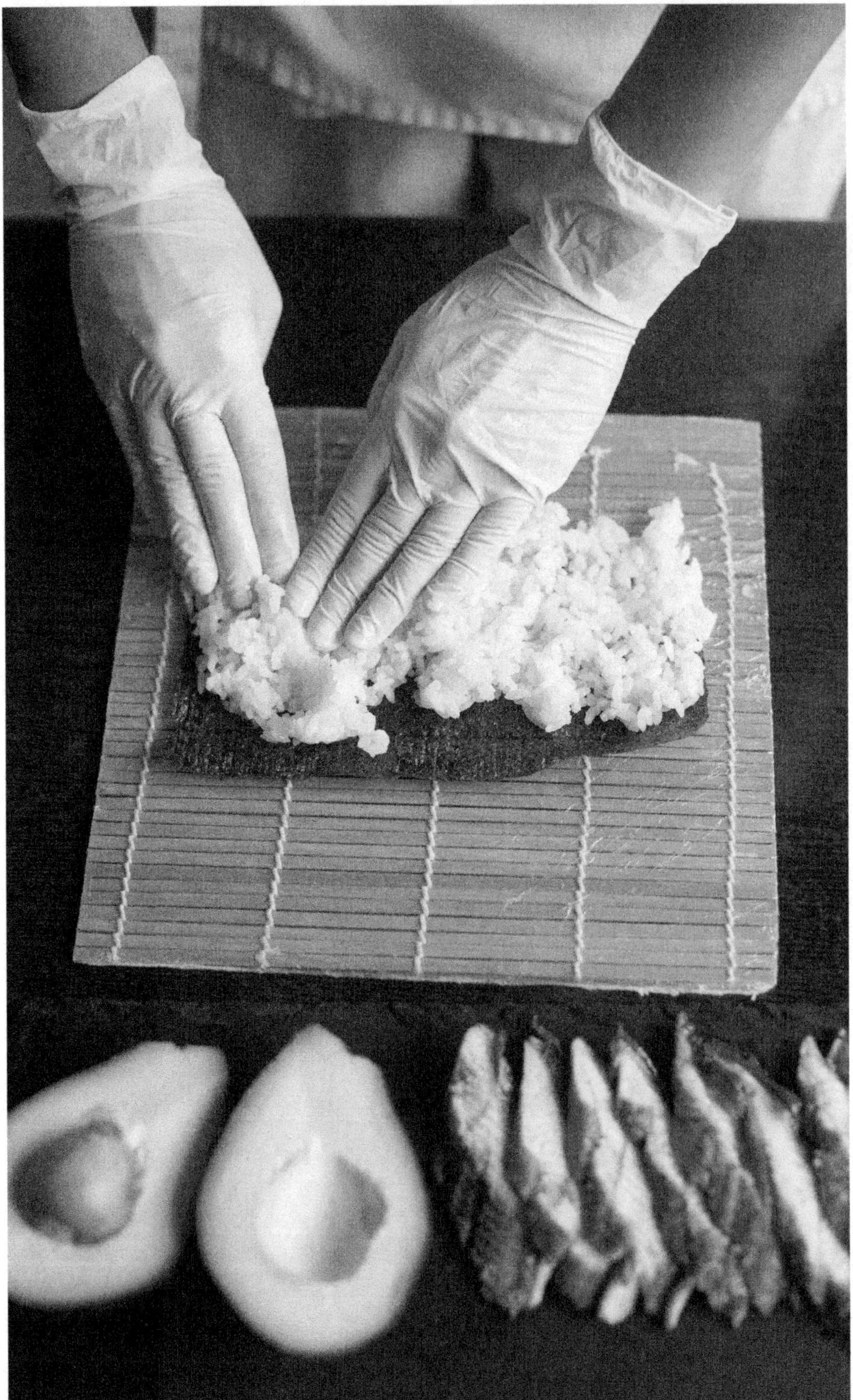

Chapter 6: Common mistakes people make when making sushi and rolls at home

Here's a list of 30 common mistakes people make when making sushi and rolls at home, along with solutions for each one to help improve your sushi-making skills!

1. Using the Wrong Type of Rice

Mistake: Using long-grain or regular rice instead of Japanese short-grain rice.
Fix: Always use short-grain rice specifically labeled "sushi rice" to achieve the right sticky texture.

2. Not Rinsing the Rice

Mistake: Skipping the rinse, which leaves excess starch, resulting in overly sticky rice.
Fix: Rinse rice thoroughly until the water runs clear to remove excess starch.

3. Incorrect Rice-to-Water Ratio

Mistake: Using too much or too little water, which leads to mushy or undercooked rice.
Fix: Use a 1:1 ratio for sushi rice and water. Adjust slightly based on your preference.

4. Skipping the Soak

Mistake: Not soaking rice before cooking, resulting in unevenly cooked rice.
Fix: Soak the rice for 20-30 minutes before cooking to ensure even texture.

5. Over-Seasoning the Rice

Mistake: Adding too much vinegar, which overpowers the rice flavor.

Fix: Use a gentle hand when adding rice vinegar. A standard ratio is 1.5 tbsp vinegar, 1 tbsp sugar, and 1/2 tsp salt per cup of uncooked rice.

6. Stirring the Rice Instead of Folding

Mistake: Stirring rice too vigorously can make it mushy and break the grains.

Fix: Use a rice paddle to gently fold the vinegar mixture into the rice.

7. Letting the Rice Dry Out

Mistake: Leaving rice uncovered, which can dry it out quickly.

Fix: Cover rice with a damp cloth to keep it moist while preparing fillings and rolling.

8. Using Hot Rice for Sushi

Mistake: Using freshly cooked, hot rice, which can cause fillings to wilt and rolls to fall apart.

Fix: Let rice cool to room temperature before using it in sushi.

9. Handling Rice with Dry Hands

Mistake: Rice sticks to hands, making it difficult to work with.

Fix: Wet your hands with water or vinegar water to prevent rice from sticking.

10. Not Using Sushi-Grade Fish

Mistake: Using non-sushi-grade fish, which may not be safe to eat raw.

Fix: Always buy sushi-grade fish from a reputable source if eating raw fish.

11. Over-Stuffing the Roll

Mistake: Adding too many fillings, making the roll difficult to close and slice.

Fix: Use small amounts of each filling to ensure a tight roll.

12. Under-Seasoning the Fish

Mistake: Not adding enough wasabi or soy sauce to enhance the fish's flavor.

Fix: Place a tiny dab of wasabi on the rice under the fish to enhance its flavor subtly.

13. Leaving the Nori Exposed to Air

Mistake: Letting nori sit out, which causes it to become chewy and lose crispness.

Fix: Keep nori in an airtight container until you're ready to use it.

14. Not Covering the Bamboo Mat with Plastic Wrap

Mistake: Rice sticks to the mat, making it difficult to roll and clean.

Fix: Wrap the mat in plastic wrap to prevent sticking.

15. Over-Packing Rice on Nori

Mistake: Adding too much rice makes the roll difficult to roll and overly thick.

Fix: Spread rice in a thin, even layer, covering about 3/4 of the nori.

16. Rolling Too Loosely

Mistake: Not applying enough pressure when rolling, which makes the roll fall apart.

Fix: Apply gentle, even pressure with the bamboo mat to achieve a tight roll.

17. Forgetting to Leave a Nori Edge for Sealing

Mistake: Spreading rice all the way to the top of the nori, making it difficult to seal.

Fix: Leave a 1-inch gap at the top edge of the nori to seal the roll easily.

18. Using a Dull Knife

Mistake: A dull knife crushes the roll and causes fillings to spill out.

Fix: Use a sharp knife for clean cuts and wet it between cuts to prevent sticking.

19. Not Chilling Fish Before Slicing

Mistake: Slicing room-temperature fish can result in uneven, messy slices.

Fix: Briefly chill fish in the freezer for about 10-15 minutes before slicing for cleaner cuts.

20. Slicing Rolls Too Thickly

Mistake: Thick slices make it hard to eat and affect presentation.

Fix: Aim for slices around 3/4 inch thick to create bite-sized pieces.

21. Neglecting to Fan the Rice for Glossiness

Mistake: Not fanning rice can make it look dull and sticky.

Fix: Fan rice while mixing in the vinegar to give it a glossy appearance.

22. Using Too Much Soy Sauce

Mistake: Dipping sushi in too much soy sauce can

overpower flavors.
Fix: Dip the fish side lightly in soy sauce, not the rice.

23. Over-Mixing Fillings in Rolls
Mistake: Overly mixing fillings like spicy tuna, which makes it mushy.
Fix: Lightly mix fillings to keep some texture.

24. Making Rolls Too Thick
Mistake: Using too much rice and filling, which makes the roll too thick to eat comfortably.
Fix: Use just enough rice to cover the nori and a modest amount of filling for a balanced roll.

25. Serving Sushi Too Cold
Mistake: Serving sushi straight from the fridge can make it less flavorful.
Fix: Let sushi rest for a few minutes at room temperature before serving.

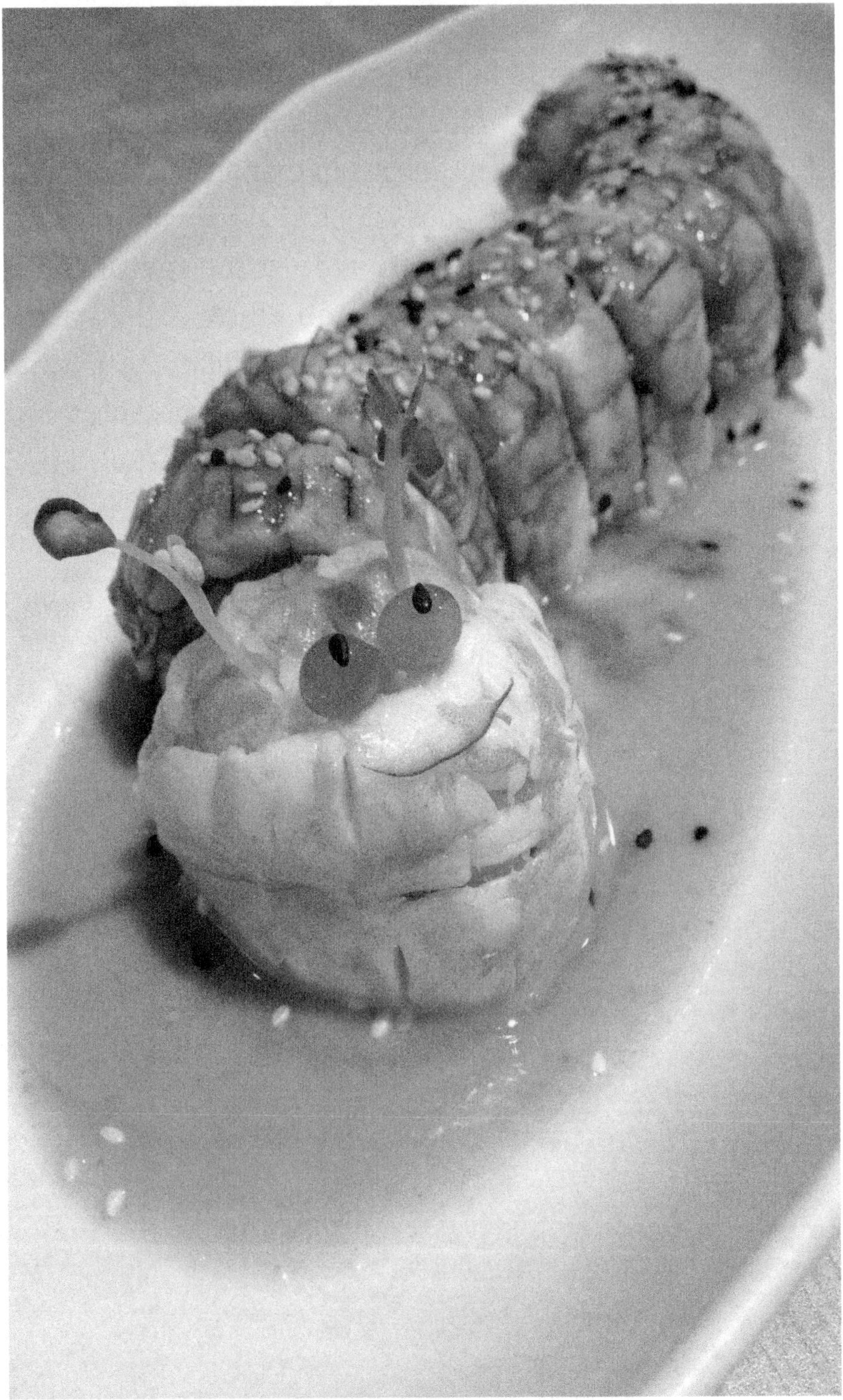

Chapter 7: Fusion Roll Recipes

Here are 10 unique and delicious fusion roll recipes that combine traditional Japanese elements with flavors from around the world.

Recipe 10: Mexican-Inspired Spicy Tuna Roll

Description: This roll combines spicy tuna with avocado, jalapeño, and a hint of lime for a fresh, zesty kick.

Ingredients:
1 cup sushi rice, prepared
1 sheet nori
100g tuna, diced
1 tbsp mayonnaise
1 tsp Sriracha
1/2 avocado, sliced
1/2 jalapeño, thinly sliced
Lime zest and juice (optional)

Method:
Mix diced tuna, mayonnaise, and Sriracha to make a spicy tuna mixture.
Lay nori on a bamboo mat, spread rice on it, flip, and add spicy tuna, avocado, and jalapeño.
Roll tightly, slice, and garnish with lime zest.
Serving Suggestion: Serve with a small dish of soy sauce and a wedge of lime.

Recipe 2: Korean BBQ Beef Roll

Description: Inspired by Korean flavors, this roll features marinated bulgogi (Korean BBQ beef), cucumber, and green onions.

Ingredients:
1 cup sushi rice, prepared
1 sheet nori
100g bulgogi beef, thinly sliced and cooked
1 cucumber, julienned
2 green onions, chopped
Sesame seeds, for garnish

Method:
Place nori on a bamboo mat, spread rice over it, flip, and add bulgogi, cucumber, and green onions.
Roll tightly, slice, and sprinkle with sesame seeds.
Serving Suggestion: Serve with a side of gochujang sauce for extra heat.

Recipe 3: California Mango Roll

Description: This roll combines the sweetness of mango with the creaminess of avocado and the fresh crunch of cucumber.

Ingredients:
1 cup sushi rice, prepared
1 sheet nori
1/2 mango, sliced
1/2 avocado, sliced
1/2 cucumber, julienned
Sesame seeds, for garnish

Method:
Place nori on the bamboo mat, spread rice, flip, and add mango, avocado, and cucumber.
Roll tightly, slice, and sprinkle with sesame seeds.
Serving Suggestion: Serve with a light drizzle of soy sauce or ponzu.

Recipe 4: Italian Caprese Roll

Description: A sushi roll inspired by the flavors of a Caprese salad with basil, fresh mozzarella, and tomato.

Ingredients:
1 cup sushi rice, prepared
1 sheet nori
4-5 basil leaves
1/2 tomato, julienned
Fresh mozzarella, cut into strips

Balsamic glaze, for drizzling

Method:
Spread rice on nori, flip, and add basil, tomato, and mozzarella.
Roll tightly, slice, and drizzle with balsamic glaze.
Serving Suggestion: Serve with a side of olive oil mixed with a hint of soy sauce.

Recipe 5: Spicy Thai Shrimp Roll
Description: This roll features shrimp with a spicy Thai-inspired peanut sauce, fresh cilantro, and crunchy carrots.

Ingredients:
1 cup sushi rice, prepared
1 sheet nori
4-5 cooked shrimp, sliced in half lengthwise
1 small carrot, julienned
Fresh cilantro leaves
1 tbsp spicy peanut sauce

Method:
Spread rice on nori, flip, and place shrimp, carrots, and cilantro.
Drizzle with peanut sauce, roll tightly, and slice.
Serving Suggestion: Serve with a small side of spicy peanut sauce for dipping.

Recipe 6: Tropical Pineapple and Shrimp Roll

Description: A fresh, tropical roll with pineapple, shrimp, and a hint of coconut for a refreshing island vibe.

Ingredients:
1 cup sushi rice, prepared
1 sheet nori
4-5 cooked shrimp
1/4 cup pineapple, diced
Shredded coconut, for garnish

Method:
Place nori on bamboo mat, spread rice, flip, add shrimp and pineapple.
Roll tightly, slice, and sprinkle with shredded coconut.
Serving Suggestion: Serve with a small side of soy sauce mixed with a splash of coconut milk.

Recipe 7:. BBQ Chicken Roll

Description: A smoky, savory roll with BBQ chicken, red bell pepper, and a drizzle of BBQ sauce.

Ingredients:
1 cup sushi rice, prepared
1 sheet nori
100g BBQ chicken, shredded
1/4 red bell pepper, thinly sliced
Green onions, chopped
BBQ sauce, for drizzling

Method:
Spread rice on nori, flip, add BBQ chicken, bell pepper, and green onions.
Roll tightly, slice, and drizzle with BBQ sauce.
Serving Suggestion: Serve with extra BBQ sauce for dipping.

Recipe 8: Buffalo Cauliflower Roll

Description: A vegan roll with crispy, spicy buffalo cauliflower and a hint of avocado to balance the heat.

Ingredients:
1 cup sushi rice, prepared
1 sheet nori
1/2 cup buffalo cauliflower (roasted or air-fried)
1/2 avocado, sliced
Green onions, for garnish

Method:
Spread rice on nori, flip, add buffalo cauliflower and avocado.
Roll tightly, slice, and sprinkle with green onions.
Serving Suggestion: Serve with vegan ranch or blue cheese dressing.

Recipe 9: Taco-Inspired Roll

Description: This roll brings taco flavors into sushi with seasoned black beans, corn, avocado, and a hint of salsa.

Ingredients:
1 cup sushi rice, prepared
1 sheet nori
1/4 cup black beans, seasoned
1/4 cup corn kernels
1/2 avocado, sliced
Salsa, for drizzling

Method:
Spread rice on nori, flip, add black beans, corn, and avocado.
Roll tightly, slice, and drizzle with a little salsa.
Serving Suggestion: Serve with extra salsa or guacamole on the side.

Recipe 10: Smoked Salmon and Cream Cheese Roll (Bagel Roll)

Description: Inspired by the classic bagel and lox, this roll combines smoked salmon, cream cheese, and a touch of dill.

Ingredients:
1 cup sushi rice, prepared
1 sheet nori
50g smoked salmon, thinly sliced
2 tbsp cream cheese
Fresh dill, for garnish

Method:
Spread rice on nori, flip, add smoked salmon and

dollops of cream cheese.
Roll tightly, slice, and garnish with fresh dill.
Serving Suggestion: Serve with a light drizzle of lemon juice or a sprinkle of capers.

These fusion rolls bring creative and unexpected flavors to traditional sushi, making them perfect for adventurous eaters or a fun sushi night with friends! Enjoy exploring these unique combinations!

Final Thoughts: Becoming a Sushi Artisan at Home

Congratulations on completing Sushi at Home: Master the Art of Sushi and Rolls! You've journeyed through the flavors, techniques, and traditions that make sushi one of the world's most beloved cuisines. You now have the knowledge to create a wide range of sushi styles, from classic nigiri and vibrant maki rolls to inventive vegetarian and baked creations. Armed with the skills you've developed, your kitchen is now a place where traditional Japanese flavors meet personal creativity.

A Few Final Tips:

Embrace the Art of Practice: Sushi-making, like any craft, improves with practice. Each roll will get a little tighter, each slice a little cleaner, and each rice mound a little closer to perfection. Let yourself enjoy the process and the learning that comes with each attempt.

Experiment and Personalize: Sushi is deeply traditional, but it's also wonderfully adaptable. Once you've mastered the basics, don't hesitate to experiment with new flavors, textures, and ingredients. Try adding your favorite flavors, like a touch of citrus zest, a drizzle of spicy mayo, or a sprinkle of sesame seeds to make each creation uniquely yours.

Share Your Creations: Sushi is a social food, made for sharing and celebrating with others. Whether you're hosting a sushi night or sharing a quiet meal with loved ones, enjoy the communal joy that sushi brings to the table.

Keep Growing: There's always more to learn. Dive deeper into Japanese cuisine, explore regional sushi variations, or hone your skills with more advanced techniques like sashimi or delicate tempura rolls. The world of sushi is rich and endless, and this book is just the beginning.

Thank you for bringing this ancient art into your home and making it part of your cooking journey. With every roll you create, you're participating in a tradition that has delighted people for centuries. So keep rolling, keep tasting, and keep sharing the joy of sushi. Here's to many more delicious creations and memories around your sushi table! Itadakimasu! Enjoy your meal, and happy sushi-making!

Printed in Great Britain
by Amazon